Copyright © 2025 June C. Porter.

All rights reserved. No part of this book may be used or reproduced by any means, graphic, electronic, or mechanical, including photocopying, recording, taping or by any information storage retrieval system without the written permission of the author except in the case of brief quotations embodied in critical articles and reviews.

Uriel Press books may be ordered through booksellers or by contacting:

Uriel Press
1663 Liberty Drive
Bloomington, IN 47403
www.urielpress.com
844-752-3114

Because of the dynamic nature of the Internet, any web addresses or links contained in this book may have changed since publication and may no longer be valid. The views expressed in this work are solely those of the author and do not necessarily reflect the views of the publisher, and the publisher hereby disclaims any responsibility for them.

Any people depicted in stock imagery provided by Getty Images are models, and such images are being used for illustrative purposes only. Certain stock imagery © Getty Images.

Scripture is taken from the King James Version, public domain.

ISBN: 979-8-8861-2034-9 (sc)
ISBN: 979-8-8861-2035-6 (hc)
ISBN: 979-8-8861-2036-3 (e)

Library of Congress Control Number: 2024906246

Print information available on the last page.

Urial Press rev. date: 04/28/2025

This Book Belongs to:

Name: _____

In Memory Of
My Husband,
Rev. Dr. Kwame John Richard Porter

My Son,
John Thomas Porter

And My Grandsons,
Jahari Jamaal Ollarvia
Jerome Marquett Porter

In Honor of My Children

Joseph Dubois Porter
Julia Magdaline Porter
Jessica Retha Houston
Jorja Angela Porter
Jerrianne Afrika Porter

In Honor of My Grand Children

Derrick Benton
Dorian Renée
Jahbril Jamaal
Jahlil Jahad
Jaryl Diallo
Jeremy Robert
Joseph Valenté
Jori Danielle
Josiah Christian
June Magdaline
Keenan Demond
Leonard Richard

In Honor of My Great Grand Children

Aiden Jerome
Janae Kamiyah
Janiyah Jade
Jaylah Elizabeth
Jerome David
Jordynn Antoinette
Josiah Christian, Jr.
Julian Andre
Kai Mark Anthony
Kingston John
Xavier Martinez

THE LORD'S PRAYER
Matthew 6:9–13
King James Version (KJV)

Our Father which art in heaven,
Hallowed be thy name.
Thy kingdom come, Thy will be done in earth, as it is in heaven.
Give us this day our daily bread.
And forgive us our debts,
as we forgive our debtors.
And lead us not into temptation,
but deliver us from evil:
For thine is the kingdom, and the power, and the glory, forever.
Amen.

Contents

I Felt Bad 2

What to Do 6

A Christmas Story 8

That Special Day 10

My Song 12

The Fight 14

My Friend 20

The Test 22

Forgiveness 26

Bored 30

Catching Up 32

Greatness in You 34

Safety 38

My Dad 40

Shh! I Hear Children Praying 41

Bedtime Prayer 43

I Felt Bad

I did something bad today, which made my mother mad.
And everybody got real quiet,
And I felt really sad.
No, I felt bad.

Nobody wanted to be with me;
I was all by myself.
I wanted to say I was sorry,
But I needed a little help.
Then I really felt bad.
No! Then I was mad.

So I pouted and fussed, and I mumbled some words.
And guess what happened? You're right—she heard!

Oh, Lord! Here she comes.
Lord, help me, I prayed.
Lord, please don't let my mama get on me today.

And my mother sat down, and she looked in my eyes.
And I was so scared—I was ready to die.

Lord, why do I do the things that I do?
I did one thing wrong, and now I've done two.

My mother looked at me and said,
"You did something bad.
That made me mad,
And so you were sad.
And then you were mad.

"But I don't feel sad,
'Cause you're not bad.
I love you."

What to Do

Jesus was born in Bethlehem many years ago.
I looked it up and heard that it's in Africa, you know.

Jesus grew and worked and lived his life across the sea.
And now, two thousand years from then, His message comes to me.

And all His life, He worked for good, way across the sea.
But I live in Chicago. What does that mean to me?

I must follow Him today.
I must show someone the way.
I must live a life that's true.
I must tell these things to you.

A Christmas Story

I saw a boy run down the street
And steal a lady's purse.

The lady cried and asked for help
And then began to curse.

That money was for Christmas gifts
And her dinner for that day.

That boy just took her money
And quickly ran away.

**Lord, help that lady understand
The meaning of Christmas this year.**

And help that boy who stole her purse to love
And cause no fear.

That Special Day

This is the day I have waited for.
It's better than Christmas for me!
Whether it's rainy or shiny,
It's the day I've waited to see.

For on that day, everybody will know,
And on the day, I really will glow.

Thank you God, for my birthday this year;
Thank you God, that my friends are near.

Thank you God, for my future in Thee;
Thank you God, for making me, ME!

My Song

As I walk to school each day,
I sing a song that goes this way:

Thank you God, that I can walk;
Thank you God, that I can talk.
Thank you—I can skip and run.
Thank you—I have lots of fun.

Thank you that my family's well;
Thank you—I can hear the bell.
Help me learn and do what's right;
Help us love and not fight.

Help me grow up tall and strong,
And let me remember this little song.

The Fight

I hit him back 'cause he hit me.
I'm not taking no hits for free.
And all the kids—they gathered round,
And then he threw me on the ground
So then I knew with all my might,
I'd have to get him; I'd have to fight.
All my friends had come to see—
Who would win, him or me?

And then I thought about my mother.
"Get him, Joe!" That was my brother.
Uh-Oh! I've got to get him down
And worry about her when I finish this clown.

Now, there we were, down in the dirt.
We were fighting hard, but I didn't feel hurt.
The kids all left 'cause they heard the bell,
And we all knew some girl would tell.

So we got up fast and stood last in line;
He was in front, and I was behind.
And he said a bad word, and he called me a name.
And I looked at him mean, and I called him the same.

And the principal called us right out of our room,
And I felt my heart go *boom, boom, boom*!
Then we went to his office and sat side by side.
And I knew it was over; I wanted to hide.

The principal picked up the phone, and I knew
He was calling my parents; I knew it was true.

Can I pray to you, Lord,
When I don't I think I'm right?
I couldn't help it; I had to fight.
Will you hear me pray, Lord, and hear me right now?
Just come in this office and help me somehow.

Then something happened, but I don't know what.
That boy started talking like some kind of nut.
He said he was sorry; he started the fight.
He didn't want his daddy to beat him that night.
So the principal hung up on whoever he was calling,

And that boy was just pleading and crying and bawling.
And I told my mother myself all about it.
I felt so happy; I wanted to shout it.
And she said she was happy it turned out that way,
But I should remember what happened that day.

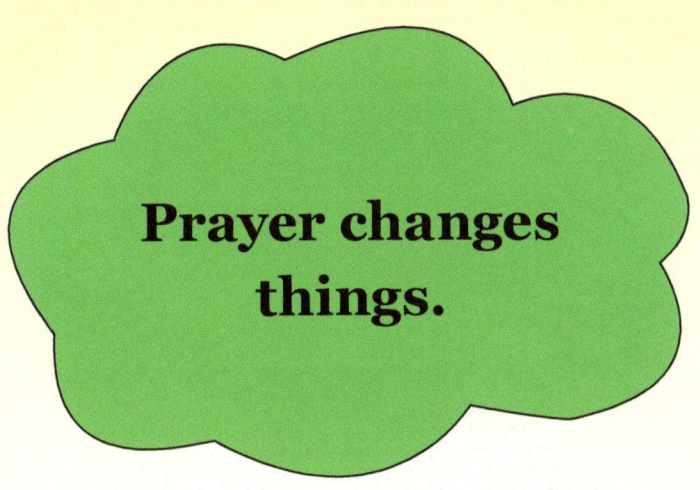

And my brother came in and said,
"Did you tell her, Joe?"
And I said, "Yeah, man, she had to know."
I prayed, **Thank you, Lord;**
The day turned out good.
I hope when I'm grown up,
I'll do as I should.

My Friend

I have a friend I really like—
At least, I think I do.
But she makes fun of old people
And wants me to do it too.

Well, I'm not doing it!
No, not me.
'Cause my great-grandmother is ninety-three.
And I've got a grandfather and two grandmothers
And aunts and uncles and lots of others.

So I told my friend to change her ways
And think of good things she could say.

Now she doesn't do that anymore,
And we're good friends just like before.

Thank you God, for friends who hear;
Thank you God, for friends so dear.

The Test

That night I studied for the test;
I knew I had to do my best.
I had to think with all my might;
I had to study hard that night.
My paper had to be real good;
It had to show all that it should.

But first I prayed: **Lord, clear my mind
And help me study well this time.**
The next day, as I took my seat,
I saw the teacher, tall and neat.

And all my classmates in the room
Sat very quietly, full of gloom.
And then I prayed before the test,
**Lord, help me pass and all the rest.
Then help our teacher, tall and neat;
Be with him as he takes his seat.
Help us write just what we know,
And help this test to make us grow.**

The room got quiet; pencils were writing.
Everyone was working; it was exciting.
Then we all stopped;
It was the bell.
Our teacher said, "I know you did well."

The next day as we entered the room,
We didn't feel nervous or full of gloom.
Our teacher said, "All the scores were high."
We all sat still and then let out a sigh.

Then I prayed,
Thank you, Lord!
Thank you, Lord, for that test.
Help us, Lord, always to
Prepare for the best!

Forgiveness

Why do I always have to forgive?
Am I supposed to get to live?
So many times, it's them, not me.
And no one else can really see
Or care
Or share.

Some folks seem to always get by
Through cheating, stealing, and even a lie.
But what can I do when it comes so close
And I feel I cannot take another dose?

Why do I always have to forgive?

I scream in anger because I'm hurt,
And I shout about their wrongs and dirt.
Then I'm blamed; the fault is on me.
They never try to feel or see
Or care
Or share.

Then I think, *When Jesus came,*
He left this world in unjust pain.
Who am I to rant and rave,
When Jesus gave and gave and gave?

Lord, help me to begin to give,
And through your death
Show how to live
And care
And share.

Jeremiah 29:11 (KJV)

For I know the thoughts that I think toward you, saith the LORD, thoughts of peace, and not of evil, to give you an expected end.

Bored

I am bored, bored, bored!
I want something fun to do.
I want something *fun* to do.

I know, I know where I can go.
I know, I know where I *must* go!

I will go into my mind;
See me look and see me find.

I will find animals no one has seen;
I'll go places no one has been.
I'll dance dances that no one has done
And draw pictures that reflect the sun.

I'll invent games no one can envision
And become a doctor with a healing incision.
I'll dream dreams that really must come true

And
I'll pray a loving prayer for you!

Catching Up

I didn't mean to shout and pout
When Mama said I couldn't go out.
I knew I hadn't done my work,
And then she said, "Sweep up this dirt.

"Take out the garbage and come right in,
And say goodbye to your friend Ken.
Tell him you'll see him in an hour or two—
If you get done all you have to do.

"We'll start on reading first today,
And then go on to math right away."
So there I was—
I couldn't go out,
Couldn't play ball. I started to pout.
I wanted to scream; I felt really mean.

My mother said, "Make up your mind.
You'll have to catch up; you're way behind."
I want to improve and do it really fast.
I want to know all I didn't get in the past.

Lord, help me learn all you need me to know,
And help me be strong in your strength as I grow.

Greatness in You
Dedicated to my late husband, Rev. Dr. Kwame John R. Porter

Some days things happen,
And I feel some kind of way.
And my feelings dictate
What I don't mean to say.

I tried to explain what I meant,
But it's too late.
The words have been heard.
I have no explanation; all my words have been blurred.

Then I think,
Do others have feelings they don't think are right
And the thoughts through their feelings keep them up at night?

My Granddad left me words that to me were new:
"Hold your head up, child;
I see greatness in you!"

When bad feelings creep in
My mind and hang around,
I call on my power to
Cut off their sound.

My power is this:
I say, "Feelings, be in control!
And all things negative
Have to unfold."

Then Father God,
My super power guides me to attack each one
And those feelings that are negative
Are gone and done.

Granddad gave me
The power today
To kill bad feelings
That come my way.

I see greatness in me
Is the power, I believe.
Anything God gives me,
I have greatness to achieve.

Safety

They laughed at me;
I didn't know why.
I was hurt and embarrassed;
I wanted to die.
One frenemy tried to hide her connection,
And not one classmate showed me affection.

I just want to crawl
Up in Jesus's arms,
Where I feel safe
And free from harm.

Where I find joy, love,
And peace overflowing
And receive his wisdom
And knowledge in knowing
That
Jesus loves me—this I know.

My Dad

I watch my dad work two jobs a day
To take care of our family
In his own special way.

My dad is smart and friendly and enjoys a good joke,
And he talks loudly and laughs
With all kinds of folks.

When we eat together and my dad prays the blessing,
I'm praying for my family
To learn God's lessons.

God, protect my dad in these unsafe streets;
Give him the desire to choose
The right foods to eat.

Help him do your work, Lord, and
Order his steps walking.
And let strong, kind words
Be heard when he's talking.

As Dad finishes the prayer,
We all say **"Amen."**
And my heart keeps praying for Dad
Forever and again.

Shh! I Hear Children Praying

I hear their voices praying today;
I hear their thoughts and some words they say.
Shh! Shh! Listen.
God, I am thankful for all
That you give,
For my parents and family,
And a place to live.

I praise you, God;
I know you are king.
I thank you, God, for everything.

Lord, sometimes I feel by myself, alone;
I even feel by myself at home.

God, help me be safe
As I walk on the street,
And give a kind spirit
To the people I meet.

These are the prayers
I've heard children say.
Shh! Shh! Listen, and you
Can hear them pray.

I thank you Lord, for giving us prayer;
I thank you Lord, because you care.

Bedtime Prayer

Now I lay me down to sleep;
I pray the Lord my soul to keep.
If I should die before I wake,
I pray the Lord my soul to take.
Bless my parents and grandparents,
My sisters and brothers,
My aunts and uncles,
My cousins,
My teachers,
My friends,
And everybody in the whole wide world.
Make me a good person.
In your name, Jesus Christ,
Forever and ever.
Amen.